GET A PARROT!

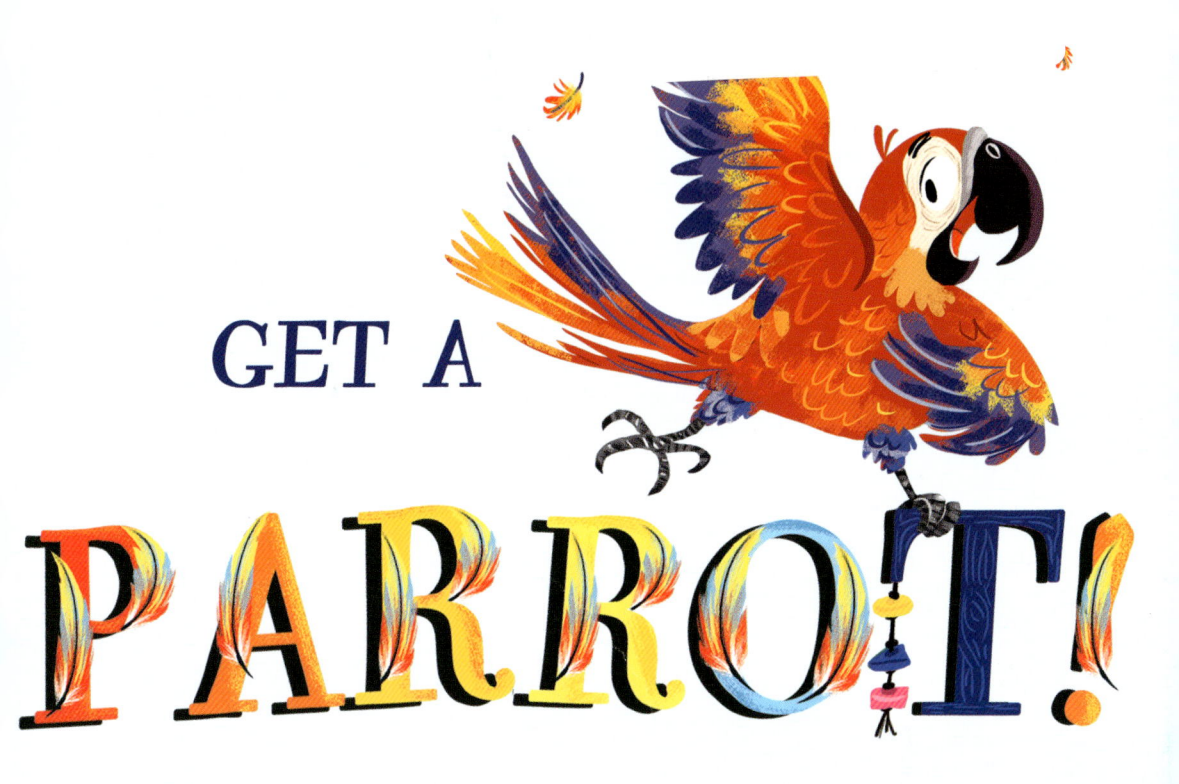

A play by Jeanne Willis

Illustrated by Nikki Dyson

Characters

Mum

Parrot

Granny

2

Dad

Sam

Pippa

Parrot: Sam and Pippa had lots of pets, but no parrot.

Sam: Mum, can we get a parrot?

Granny: Get a parrot!

Mum: No, you have lots of pets!

Dad: Yes, you have a cat, a rabbit, three hens and a goat.

Mum: You do not need a parrot as well.

Pippa: But parrots are cool!

Parrot: Dad did not think so.

Dad: Parrots peck things and make a mess.

Sam: I will clear up the mess, Dad.

Granny: Get a parrot! Get a parrot!

Parrot: Mum did not want a parrot.

Mum: Parrots cost a lot of money.

7

Pippa: I will pay for the parrot, Mum.

Sam: And I will help. Please can we have a parrot?

Pippa: Yes, please?

Granny: Get a parrot!

Parrot: The kids went on and on. So did Granny.

Sam: Mum, can we have a parrot? Please?

Mum: No! We are not having a parrot!

Pippa: Dad, can we have a parrot? Please?

Dad: I told you – no!

Granny: Get a parrot! Get a parrot!

Parrot: Mum and Dad got fed up. They had a think.

Mum: The kids are very good with pets.

Dad: Perhaps we can get them a dog.

Granny: Get a parrot.

Mum: Granny, you are not helping.

Parrot: They all went to the pet shop to look at some dogs.

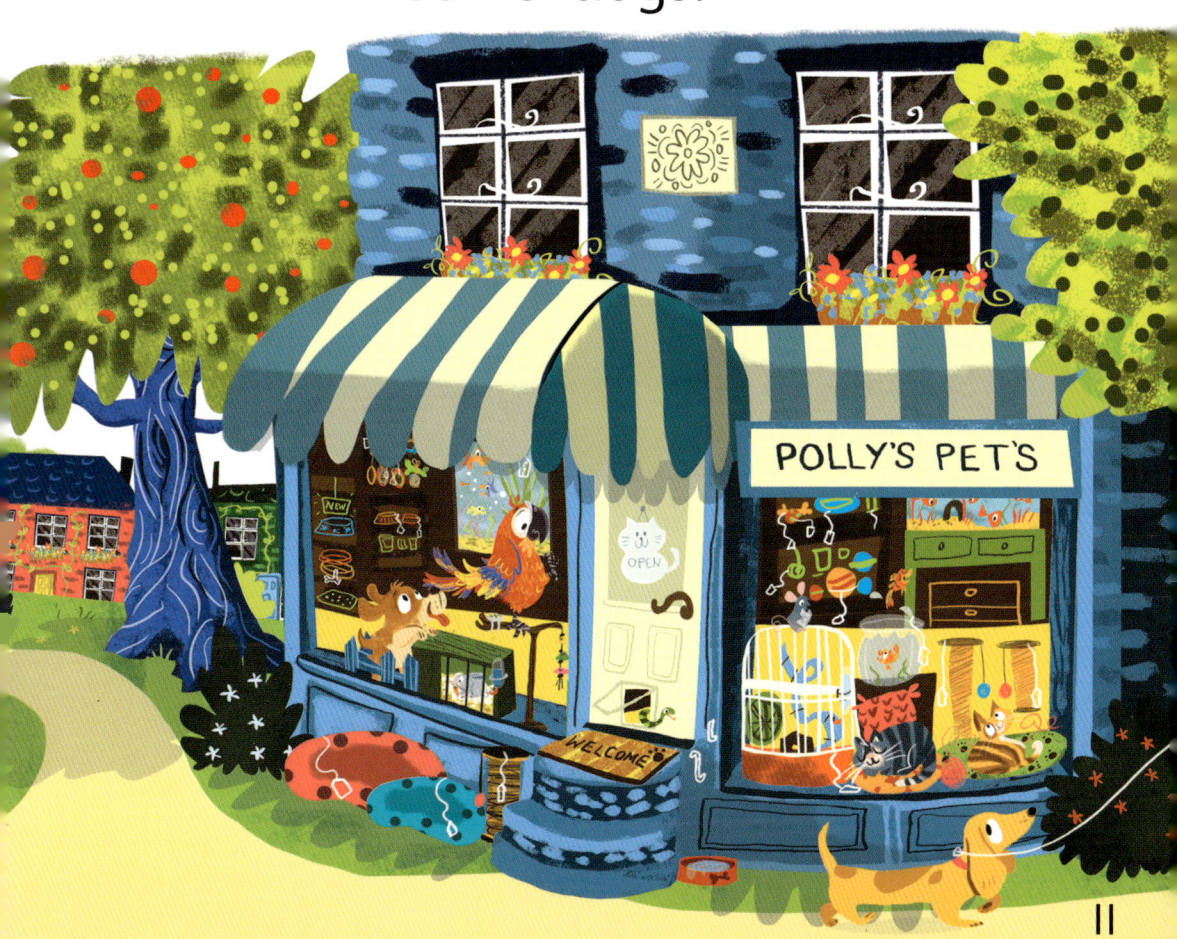

Mum: That dog is very sweet.

Sam: It's okay.

Parrot: GET A PARROT! GET A PARROT!

Mum: Granny, you are not helping!

Granny: That was not me. It was that parrot!

Pippa: It can say things!

Dad: Gosh! What a clever parrot!

Parrot: Mum and Dad had a think.

Mum: The kids will go on and on until we get that parrot.

Dad: So will Granny.

Mum: And now the parrot is nagging us too!

Dad: It is a very clever parrot! Okay – let's get it.

CUTE

Granny whispers to Sam and Pippa.

Granny: I had to keep coming to the shop to train the parrot!

Sam: Nice one, Granny!

Parrot: Who's a clever girl, then?

Granny: I am!